CURIOUS CATS

Christmas- 1996
from
Ann & Dennis

CURIOUS CATS

Edited by Morag Neil

RIZZOLI
NEW YORK

First published in the United States of America in 1996 by
RIZZOLI INTERNATIONAL PUBLICATIONS, INC.
300 Park Avenue South, New York, NY 10010

First published in the UK in 1996 by
New Holland (Publishers Ltd

ISBN 0-8478-1941-8

LC 95-72949

Editorial Direction: Yvonne McFarlane
Designer: Peter Crump
Special photography: Shona Wood
Text researcher: Joanna Ryde
Craft designs and additional illustrations:
Labeena Ishaque based on ideas by Juliet Bawden

Reproduction by Hirt and Carter,
Cape Town, South Africa
Printed and bound in Singapore by
Tien Wah Pres (Pte) Ltd

Contents

$\mathcal{A}ristocats$

CATS ARE mysterious beings... symbols of
evil, gods of the Pharaohs. You never know
if they love you or if they condescend to
occupy your house. This mystery is what
makes them the most attractive beast.

PAUL MORE
Episcopal bishop of New York
(1864-1937)

*T*HERE are no ordinary cats

COLETTE (1873-1954)

*W*HO can believe that
there is no soul behind
Those luminous eyes?

THÉOPHILE GAUTIER (1811-72)

For I rejoice in my cat Matty.
For his coat is variegated in black and
        brown, with white undersides.
For in every way his whiskers are
        marvellous.

GAVIN EWART (1916-95)
Collected Poems

SUCH SINGING – prettier than any words –

O singers you are sweet and well-to-do!

My cat, who has the finest taste in birds,

Thinks so too

D. S. MACCOLL (1859-1948)
Connoisseurs

*I*F A FISH is the movement of water
embodied, given shape, then a cat is
a diagram and pattern of subtle air.

DORIS LESSING (1919-)

The White Cat

I AM the cat of cats. I am
The everlasting cat!
Cunning, and old, and sleek as jam,
The everlasting cat!

WILLIAM BRIGHTY RANDS (1823-82)
The Cat of Cats

*I*N Ancient Egypt, they were
worshipped as gods. This makes
them too prone to set themselves
up as critics and censors of the
frail and erring human beings
whose lot they share.

P.G. WODEHOUSE
(1881–1975)

Oriental Cats Frieze

$\mathcal{M}$AKE A stencil by transferring this cat design onto a large piece of stencil card. Carefully cut out the design with a craft knife. You can, of course, enlarge or reduce it in size, depending on how you plan to use the design.

$\mathcal{U}$SE LOW-TACK masking tape to secure the stencil card to the surface you wish to paint; this will prevent it slipping while you work.

$\mathcal{A}$PPLY THE paint with a sponge, using light, dabbing strokes. You might wish to practise on a separate piece of paper before you start to paint the actual design.

$\mathcal{V}$ARY THE density of the colour, if you like, graduating from a dark brown at the bottom to a lighter shade in the middle.

$\mathcal{C}$HANGE to a soft yellow and finish off the tops of the tail, face and ears. Leave for a few seconds, then peel off the masking tape and move the stencil along, lining it up carefully. Leave a little space between each cat, tape the stencil down again and repeat the process to create a frieze.

$\mathcal{W}$HEN THE design is quite dry, you can always apply a light coat of matt varnish to the finished stencil for added protection.

Good Companions

$\mathcal{S}$TATELY, kindly, lordly friend,

Condescend

Here to sit by me, and turn

Glorious eyes that smile and burn,

Golden eyes, love's lustrous meed,

On the golden page I read.

ALGERNON CHARLES SWINBURNE (1837-1909)
To a Cat

$\mathcal{L}$IKE THOSE great sphinxes lounging through eternity

In noble attitudes upon desert sand

Cats gaze incuriously at nothing, calm and wise.

CHARLES BAUDELAIRE (1821-67)
Les Fleurs du Mal

*ℰ*VEN THE most overweight cats
instinctively know the cardinal rule: When fat,
arrange yourself in slim poses.

JOHN WEITZ (1923-)

"... *I* will eat first and wash my face afterwards."

Which all cats do, even to this day.

CHARLES H. ROSS
The Book of Cats : A Chit-Chat Chronicle
(1868)

LIFE will go on for ever,
With all that cat can wish;
Warmth, and the glad procession
Of fish, and milk and fish.

Only – the thought disturbs him –
He's noticed once or twice,
The times are somehow breeding
A nimbler race of mice.

ALEXANDER GRAY (1882-1968)
On a Cat, Aging

CATS are intended to teach us
that not everything in nature has a function.

GARRISON KEILLOR (1942-)

CATS can be very funny, and have the oddest
ways of showing they're glad to see you.

W. H. AUDEN (1907-73)

*T*HE CAT is a dilettante in fur.

THEOPHILE GAUTIER (1811-72)

I ALLOW my cats to express themselves, never
interfere with their romances and raise them with
dogs to broaden their outlook.

MURRAY ROBINSON

Cute Cats Gift Tags

USING THE photograph as a guide, draw a simple cat outline onto watercolour paper or thin, white card. Carefully cut around the outline, with scissors, and a craft knife for the more detailed cutting.

FOR THE cat's body, use a brush and oil pastels to blend the colours and make stripes and patches, then draw the face details with coloured crayons, and shadow in the ear and leg areas.

MAKE a small hole using a thick needle. Make ties from short pieces of fine ribbon or cord and thread through the holes. Repeat with a variety of colours to make gift tags of your choice.

Creatures
of Comfort

CATS sleep
Anywhere,
Any table,
Any chair.
Top of piano,
Window-ledge,
In the middle,
On the edge. ...

ELEANOR FARJEON
(1881-1965)
Cats

*H*E BLINKS upon the hearth-rug
And yawns in deep content,
Accepting all the comforts
That Providence has sent.

J. R. R. TOLKEIN
(1892-1973)
Cat

*W*HEN I play with my cat

Who knows whether she is not amusing herself

with me more than I with her?

MICHEL DE MONTAIGNE
(1533-92)
Essais

Louder he purrs, and louder,
In one glad hymn of praise,
For all the night's adventures,
For quiet, restful days.

J. R. R. TOLKEIN
(1892-1973)
Cat

*U*NDER the leaves
Of a morning glory:
Cat's eyes.

NATSUME SOSEKI (1867-1916)
Zen Haiku

$\mathcal{W}$HILE lean old Hans he snores away

Till peep of light at break of day;

Then he climbs up to his creaking mill.

Out come his cats all gray with meal – Jekkel and

Jessup, and one-eyed Jill.

WALTER DE LA MARE (1873-1956)
Five Eyes

A LITTLE drowsing cat
is an image
of perfect beautitude.

CHAMPFLEURY (JULES FL.-HUSSON)
(1821-89)

Cat's Paw Collars

MAKE A designer collar for your cat using
a length of thin fabric lined with felt, or buy a
collar from a pet store and decorate it yourself
using waterproof fabric paints.

BECAUSE most cat collars are quite narrow,
you will need to choose a very fine paint
brush to work with.

SELECT PLAIN black fabric paint or mix brown
and black or black and white for a lighter

colour. Alternatively, instead of using paint and a paintbrush, you could work the design with a marker pen, the shade of your choice.

*A*T REGULAR intervals along the length of the collar, paint tiny triangles and add four dots to each one to simulate a cat's footprint.

*Y*OU CAN always make your own variations based on this design using, for example, a variety of alternating shades. This cat's paw motif will also look well on a cat's lead, if you use one: a matching lead and collar would make an unusual present for any fashion-conscious cat!

Curiouser and Curiouser

Top Cats

BRITAIN'S	AMERICA'S
Persian	*Persian*
Siamese	*Maine Coon*
Shorthair	*Siamese*
Burmese	*Abyssinian*
Birman	*Scottish Fold*

THE world's first green cat has been found in Denmark. The little kitten, whose fur and even claws are green, was discovered near a hay barn in the northwest of the country. Its strange appearance may be a local phenomenon linked to water from corroded copper pipes – in the same area several blonde women's hair has also turned green.

THE OLDEST cat in the world was reputedly 34-year-old Ma, a female tabby from Devon, England.

*P*ROBABLY the most intrepid cat was
a tiny Swiss kitten whose owner lived in
Geneva. This four-month old trainee climber
followed a party of mountaineers to the summit of
the Matterhorn, one of the world's highest mountains.

*O*VER 100 cat breeds are now recognized
throughout the world. Most breeds date
back to around a century ago, when cats
were first formally mated to breed
animals with particular
charateristics – colour
and shape of eyes; hair
colour, length and pattern;
body shape and personality.

Sweet Dreams

*I*N THE FIRST few weeks of their lives, very young kittens spend 80 per cent of their slumbering hours in deep sleep. While they may look sweet, it is unwise to wake a kitten, for like humans, they need their dreamworld if they are to stay physically and mentally healthy.

*T*HE AVERAGE cat sleeps about 16 hours a day and in the wild only sloths sleep longer (around 19 hours).

*F*ELINE sleeping patterns change according to the seasons. All cats are more active in the spring and summertime when some outdoor cats hunt for up to 12 hours a day.

*C*ATS BEGIN their slumber with a 30-minute period of motionless, light sleep when the brainwaves are slow and the cat is slightly aware of its surroundings. This is followed by the all-important, 6-8-minute deep sleep when it will probably dream as it stretches out and rolls on its side, completely relaxed before emerging through more light sleep and becoming fully awake.

*C*ATS PROBABLY spend around three hours a day in deep, "rapid eye movement sleep". This compares with reptiles and fish who have no similarly discernible phase or rats with around 30 minutes daily and birds around 30 seconds!

A Cat by Any Other Name

ARABIC *Kitte*

ARMENIAN *Gatz*

BASQUE *Catua*

CHINESE *Miu or mio*

DANISH *Kat*

DUTCH *Kat*

HINDI *Billi*

FINNISH *Kissa*

FRENCH *Chat*

GERMAN *Katti, ket or katze*

GREEK *Gatta*

ICELANDIC *Kottur*

ITALIAN *Gatto*

JAPANESE *Neko*

LATIN *Felis or cattus*

NORWEGIAN *Gatt*

POLISH *Kott*

PORTUGUESE *Gato*

RUSSIAN *Kotz or koshka*

SPANISH *Gato*

SWEDISH *Katt*

Mischievous as Kittens

$\mathcal{A}$ KITTEN is so flexible that she is almost double; the hind parts are equivalent to another kitten with which the forepart plays. She does not discover that her tail belongs to her until you tread on it.

HENRY DAVID THOREAU
(1817-62)

PASSING year
Our cat plays
By the water

CHUHO KEIDO
(1860-1912)
Haiku

IT's TOO deep
To go across, besides
I can't swim.

NETSUME SOSEKI
(1867-1916)
Zen Haiku

After the butterfly's gone
It settles down:
A kitten.

NETSUME SOSEKI
(1867-1916)
Zen Haiku

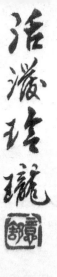

"*I*T IS A VERY inconvenient habit of kittens," said Alice,
"that whatever you say to them, they always purr."

*T*HEY HAD dear little fur coats of their own;
and they tumbled about the doorstep
and played in the dust.

BEATRIX POTTER (1866-1943)
The Tale of Tom Kitten

Fishes Cat Bowl

*Y*OU CAN customize any bowl of your choice using non-toxic, waterbased, cold ceramic paints. With a wax pencil or a marking pen, draw fish shapes around the outer rim of the bowl and one in the middle inside it, then add fish bones around the inner rim.

*U*SING A fine paint brush, carefully paint the blue fish bone design along the inner rim of the bowl. To make it easier to produce steady brush strokes, place the bowl on its side and paint with your hand resting on a firm surface.

*A*LLOW TO DRY – this can take a couple of hours – then dot in the eyes with gold paint. Create the fish shapes around the outside of the bowl with gold paint. Fill in with more of the same paint and allow to dry.

*N*OW USE THE blue paint to add the criss-cross patterns and dot in the eyes. Allow to dry completely and finish off inside and out with non-toxic ceramic glaze.

Small Wild Beasts

*T*EARAWAY kitten or staid mother of fifty
Persian, Chinchilla, Siamese
Or backstreet brawler – you all have a tiger in your blood
And eyes as opaque as the sacred mysteries.

CECIL DAY LEWIS (1904-72)
Cat

I SAW the most beautiful cat today. It was sitting by the side of
the road, its two front feet neatly and graciously together. Then
it gravely swished around its tail to completely and snugly
encircle itself. It was so fit and beautifully neat, the gesture,
and so self-satisfied - so complacent.

ANNE MORROW LINDBERGH

A CAT who has taken umbrage

is a terrible sight to see.

ROSEMARY NISBET (1923-79)
Cats' Lives, 1970

𝒲HISKER and claw, they crouch in the night,
Their fine eyes smouldering

Green and bright...
Squeaking and scampering everywhere.
Then they pounce, now in, now out,
At whisking tail and sniffing snout...

WALTER DE LA MARE (1873-1956)
Five Eyes

$\mathcal{T}$HEY call me cruel. Do I know if mouse or songbird feels?
I only know they make me light and salutary meals.
And if, as 'tis my nature to, ere I devour I tease 'em.
Why should a low-bred gardener's boy pursue me
with a besom?

C.S. CALVERLEY (1831-84)
Sad Memories, 1862

He REJOICES with quick leaps
When in his sharp claw sticks a mouse:
I too rejoice when I have grasped
A problem difficult and dearly loved.

Pangur Ban
Ancient Irish Poetry (8TH CENT. AD)

Catnip Mice

CUT A PIECE OF material into a circle measuring 9½ in (24 cm) in diameter; cut into four quarters. Take one of the pieces and, with the right sides facing, fold the fabric with the straight edges together. Using small, tight running stitches, sew these edges together and turn the right way out, to produce a cone shape.

SEW A LINE of loose running stitches around the opening of the base. Pack the mouse with every cats' favourite herb, catnip. Draw up the running stitches at the base and tie the ends to close the body.

FOR THE TAIL, cut a strip of leather or shoe lace and stitch onto the body closing. Cut out a small circle of the same fabric and use fabric glue to attach it to the rear of the mouse; this will hide the stitching.

TO MAKE THE ears, cut out two small circles of brown felt. Stitch tightly onto each side of the head, gathering the bottom of the circle slightly. Use black thread to stitch in eyes, nose and whisker details. Repeat the process with the other fabric quarters, if you wish to make several mice.

The Artist's Cat

*T*HE CAT went here and there
And the moon spun round
like a top.
And the nearest kin of the moon,
The creeping cat,
looked up.

W.B. YEATS (1865-1939)
The Cat and the Moon

"PLEASE would you tell me," said Alice a little timidly, for she was not quite sure whether it was good manners for her to speak first, "why your cat grins like that!"

"It's a Cheshire cat," said the Duchess, "and that's why."

"I didn't know that Cheshire cats always grinned; in fact, I didn't know that cats could grin."

"They all can, and most of 'em do," said the
Duchess looking at the cat in the bough of a
tree a few yards off. The cat only grinned when
it saw Alice. It looked good natured, she
thought, as the Cheshire-Puss vanished quite
slowly, beginning with the end of the tail, and
ending with the grin, which remained some
time after the rest of it had gone.

LEWIS CARROLL (1832-98)
Alice's Adventures in Wonderland, 1865

$\mathcal{P}$LUMP NECK, short ears, height
to his head proportionate;
Beneath his ebony nostrils
His little leonine muzzle's
Prim beauty, which appeared
Fringed by the silvery beard
Which gave such waggish grace
To his young dandy's face.

JOACHIM DU BELLAY (1525-60)
Epitaph on a Pet Cat

CAT. n.f. [*katz*, Teuton, *chat*, Fr] A domestick
animal that catches mice, commonly reckoned by
naturalists the lowest order of the leonine species.

DR SAMUEL JOHNSON (1709-1884)
A Dictionary of the English Language

EVERYTHING a cat is
and does physically
is to me beautiful, lovely,
stimulating, soothing, attractive and
and enchantment.

PAUL GALLICO (1897-1976)
An Honourable Cat

WITH a tiger-leap half way
Now she meets the coming prey,
Lets it go as fast, and then
Has it in her power again:
Now she works with three or four,
Like an Indian conjurer....

WILLIAM WORDSWORTH (1770-1850)
The Kitten and Falling Leaves

Decoupaged Lamp and Shade

Either DRAW, photocopy or trace illustrations which have a strong outline and cut out as many shapes as you wish to use. If tracing, do this on black paper.

Arrange THE cat shapes around the base of the shade and stick them into position with white glue.

For THE lamp base, draw the outlines of paw prints onto it using a wax pencil. If you make any errors you can always rub out the outlines and start again.

When YOU are happy with the positioning of the paws, fill in the design using a fine paint brush and black acrylic paint. You can make the footprints as sparse or dense as you like.

⤳ Acknowledgements

The Publishers would like to thank The
Bridgeman Art Library (BAL), E.T.Archive (ETA),
AKG London (AKG), Visual Arts Library (VAL),
Mary Evans Picture Library (MEPL), Christies
Images (CI), The Mercury Gallery (TMG), British
Museum (BM), Central Illustration Agency (CIA),
Jean-Loup Charmet (JLC), Explorer, Paris (E),
Bildarchiv Pressischer Kulturbesitz, Berlin (BPK),
The Image Bank (IB), SuperStock (S) for their
assistance and loan of the pictures included in
this book.

Front cover, *Three Friends on Kasai Mat*/Derold
Page (BAL); back cover, *Sam the All -American
Cat*/Robert McCauley (ETA); half title, Ronald
Searle; frontispiece, *Cat on a rug*/Elizabeth
Blackadder (CI); 6, cat sun-god (BM); 7, Egyptian
bronze cat/Margarete Büsing (© BPK);
8, © Cambazard (E); 9, engraving/Martin Leman;
10, *Cats*/Micha Koeck (AKG); 11, *Cat Fantasy*
(JLC); 12, *The White Cat*/E. Mackinstry (ETA);
13, *Puss-in-Boots* poster (ETA); 14, Egyptian
sculpture/Margarete Büsing (© BPK); 15, *Siamese
Cats* lithograph/Jacques Nam (ETA); 18, *Jack
Russell and Persian*/F. Rutherford (ETA);
19, *Beyond the Ilex*/Derold Page, (BAL); 20, *On the
Mat*/Jerzy Marek (BAL); 21, *Tom, Dick and
Henry*/Derold Page (BAL); 22, *Puss the Cat* (BAL);
23, *Lait de la Vingeanne* (JLC); 24, cats eating
meat pie (ETA); 25, cat playing banjo/Ernest
Nister (ETA); 26, *A Persian Cat and Her
Kittens*/Maud D. Heaps (BAL); 27, Ronald Searle;
30, *Sandy*/Martin Leman; 31, *The Calico Cat's
Dream*/Derold Page (BAL); 32, *Tinkie*/Derold Page
(BAL); 33, *Nerissa*/Joan Freestone (BAL); 34, *Cat
on a Yellow Pillow*/Franz Marc (AKG); 35, *Sleeping
Cat*/Japanese watercolour (BAL); 36, *Old Mr
Tombs*/Ditz (BAL); 37, *Creatures of Comfort*/Alice
Woodhuysen (BAL); 45, *Flying Kitties*/Pierre (S);
46, *Kitten and wool*/Murata Kokodu, 1866 (ETA);
47, *Kitten with Butterfly*/Chinese embroidery
(BAL); 48, Catland acrobats (ETA); *Cat with
Strawberry*/Martin Leman; 49, *L'accident*/David
Merlin (VAL); 52, *Cat and Mouse*/Ken Joudrey
(IB); 53, Imafrei Russe J. L. Charmet/Explorer (E);
54, tiled panel, Lisbon (ETA); 55, tiled panel,
Lisbon (ETA); 56, *Still Life with Cat and Mouse*
(BAL); 57, Kalighat/Victoria & Albert Museum,
London (ETA); 58, Roman mosaic (AKG);
59, *The Town Mouse and Country Mouse*/Kay
Nielsen (ETA); 62, Franz Marc (AKG); 63, *Cat in
Variation*/Fred Bornet (IB); 64, *Alice and the
Cheshire Cat*/Tenniel (MEPL); 65, *The Cheshire
Cat Reappears*/Tenniel (MEPL); 67, *The Gourmet
Cat*/Ronald Searle (AKG); 68, *Cat and Fiddle*
/Andrew Kulman (CIA); 69, Andrew Kulman
(CIA).

The Publishers have made every effort to identify
copyright holders of material included in this book
and apologize for any inadvertent omissions, which
they will rectify in the event of a reprint.